Camino Quick Guide

Walking the French Way of Saint James
Year 2024

Juan Martín García

Camino Quick Guide
Juan Martín García © 2024 Spain
info@atc-innova.com
Translator: Al Thibeault
Reviewer: Eva Méndez Alonso

The book is based on the experiences and opinions of the author, and is not intended as recommendations to the readers, who must evaluate their own circumstances. This document may not be copied, reproduced, transmitted or otherwise distributed, in whole or in part, in digital, electronic, paper or any other format, without the prior written consent of the Copyright.

Index

Preface 7

1. The Way of Saint James 9

History
The Camino today
Pilgrim or tourist, walker
Routes to Compostela
The stages
Types of roads

2. Make the decision (6 months before) 23

The reason
Which route to choose
Books and guides
Alone or accompanied
Budget
In summary: yes or no

3. Planning (3 months before) 37

Starting point
The start date
Plan the stages
Accommodations

4. Preparations (1 month before) 47

Test routes
Clothing and footwear
Backpack and cane
Luggage
Mobile and camera
Pilgrim's Credential
Take care

5. Running (1 day before)   63

The first day
Some things to do

6. The stages   69

A personal experience
Some things that happen

7. The French Camino   77

Distances
Accommodations visited
Stages
1. Roncesvalles - Burguete
2. Burguete - Zubiri
3. Zubiri - Pamplona
4. Pamplona - Puente la Reina
5. Puente la Reina - Estella
6. Estella - Los Arcos
7. Los Arcos - Viana
8. Viana - Logroño
9. Logroño - Nájera
10. Nájera - Santo Domingo de la Calzada
11. Santo Domingo de la Calzada - Belorado
12. Belorado - Agés
13. Agés - Burgos
14. Burgos - Hontanas
15. Hontanas - Boadilla del Camino
16. Boadilla - Carrión de los Condes
17. Carrión de los Condes - Terradillos
18. Terradillos - El Burgo Ranero
19. El Burgo - Mansilla de las Mulas
20. Mansilla de las Mulas - León
21. León - San Martín del Camino
22. San Martín del Camino - Astorga
23. Astorga - Rabanal del Camino

24. Rabanal del Camino - El Acebo
25. El Acebo - Ponferrada
26. Ponferrada - Villafranca del Bierzo
27. Villafranca del Bierzo - Las Herrerías
28. Las Herrerías - O Cebreiro
29. O Cebreiro - Triacastela
30. Triacastela - Sarria
31. Sarria - Portomarín
32. Portomarín - Palas de Rei
33. Palas de Rei - A Fraga Alta
34. A Fraga Alta -O Pedrouzo
35. O Pedrouzo - Santiago de Compostela

8. The Compostela   159

9. To be continued   163

10. Acknowledgments   167

11. Basic vocabulary   171

12. My own notes   177

Preface

The Way of Saint James, also called the 'Camino de Santiago' or the 'Camino', is a crazy but rewarding adventure. For readers who are considering it, this book will be a help to make an informed decision and then plan it well.

To do the Camino is to walk, nothing more. Walking is not running or climbing, but neither is it strolling at the mall.

This guide is based on my experience of having completed the Camino from Roncesvalles to Santiago de Compostela walking about 500 miles in 35 days, and having finished better than I was at the beginning.

Buen Camino !

1. The Way of Saint James

In the mists of dawn inhabit the souls of the pilgrims
who for centuries have traveled to Santiago

History

There is much history, myth and legend about the Camino. Most believe that in the year 813 the tomb of the apostle Santiago el Mayor (St. James the Great) was discovered in the crypt of the current Cathedral of Santiago de Compostela. Tradition says that the apostle Santiago was preaching in Galician lands until his death. Eight centuries later, at the beginning of the Reconquest, a hermit saw a star lodged in the forest of Libredón, and when going to the place with the bishop of Padrón they found a small chapel and, inside, a tomb that they attributed to the apostle Santiago. They called that place Compostela (from the Latin Campus Stellae, the field of stars). Then, King Alfonso II of Asturias visited the place and ordered the building of a church over the chapel. Gradually and over time, pilgrims from all over Europe began to arrive in Compostela, and by the 11th century it was becoming a habitual pilgrimage. Much later, in the time of the Catholic Monarchs (during the 15th century), the city of Santiago de Compostela became, along with Rome and Jerusalem, one of the « three great pilgrimages in Christianity ». With the conferral of Pope Alexander VI the 16th century became the period of greatest splendor of Compostela.

During the following centuries the number of pilgrims diminished. This is attributed to famines, epidemics, and the wars that often shake Europe. The Compostela was falling into oblivion. Much later, 19th century, during the War of Independence much of the heritage was destroyed and plundered. Fortunately, the well kept humble bones of the Saint were saved from pillaging, and today are venerated by the faithful of the five continents.

The towns that mark the route are oases
to rest and recover one's strength.

The Camino today

The revitalization of the Camino de Santiago started in 1993 with the Holy Year of Compostela. With a good promotional campaign and the collaboration of the government the infrastructure along the route was improved. The result is that the number of walkers grew from about 5,000 people per year to almost 100,000 people in the year 1993. This growth has continued and has reached 300,000 people annually today.

This might give the impression that there are too many people, but if we distribute them over 300 days and the 800 kilometers from Roncesvalles to Santiago de Compostela, we see that they would be separated from each other by over one kilometer. The Camino is a busy place, but in no way saturated.

Today the route is through rural roads, narrow and steep paths, and sometimes a roadside. It has good accommodations and catering services, which allow the walker to combine the solitary tranquility of a walk through the fields and mountains with the security of others always being nearby.

Without a doubt, doing the Camino is a different experience for each person. For those who complete it, it is always a very rewarding experience.

This guide is intended for people with no serious health ailments or demanding obligations. You must examine if your motivation is powerful enough, and if so, how to plan the walk in the best possible way.

For all walkers it is an adventure,
for pilgrims it is also a penance

Pilgrim or tourist, walker

Each person who travels on the Camino de Santiago has their own reasons. In general there are two main groups of walkers: pilgrims and tourists.

Pilgrims are those who embark on this adventure for religious reasons such as penance. The pilgrim archetype, with infinite nuances, is a person who is not used to playing sports, has little interest in the culture or history of the places on the Camino, and with the clear and single goal of reaching the Santiago de Compostela. Pilgrims take the inevitable hardships of the journey as an additional penance. The physiotherapists who attend to the pilgrims often hear them say « suffering for Christ is a privilege. » Theirs is a tour of cathedrals, churches and hermitages that concludes at the usual Mass of 7:00 in the evening. We will find here Spanish, Asian, American and European pilgrims, all united by the same faith.

Tourists are all the other people. They are those who want to enjoy a few days in the country, have some physical exercise, but with the safety of a busy route and good services. With many nuances, they do some sports regularly, they want to enjoy a humble omelet in the middle of a wasteland, the history hidden in each bridge, and different cultures. They do not appreciate suffering as a merit.

Another distinction is that pilgrims exult at reaching Santiago de Compostela and achieving their religious goal, while tourists feel rather melancholy, as for them an adventure is coming to an end. To simplify here we will call them collectively « walkers », to describe both pilgrims and tourists.

Cities receive walkers and offer
them their history and culture

Routes to Compostela

For those who wish to make the Camino as a pilgrimage, it is important to understand that the Camino begins and ends at the door of their house, from where they must leave and to where they must return. Along the way it is easy to encounter fellow walkers following this notion. Throughout the centuries, routes have been defined, based on the location of the cities and the orography.

The most important routes had their start in the French cities of Paris, Vézelay, Puy-en-Velay and Arles, across the Pyrenees at Roncesvalles or Canfranc, united again at Puente la Reina and from there through Logroño, Burgos and León and finally arriving at Santiago de Compostela.

Today there are innumerable Jacobean (Jacob is the original Hebrew form of the Latin name James) routes to choose from, which depart from almost anywhere in Europe. In Spain you can find well-marked routes from Cádiz, Málaga, Castellón, Tarragona, Jaén, Madrid, Seville, etc. on which it is easy to find directions. Each route has its own name: «Camino Primitivo», «Mozarabic route to Santiago», «Camino Levantino», «Camino de Santiago de la Lana», etc.

The busiest route, and the one that has better services and that the author has traveled, starts in Roncesvalles, and it is known as the «French Way». It is not the purpose of this book to compare the routes and recommend one; each has its merits. In any case it seems prudent to opt for the route that offers more rather than fewer services, and this, without a doubt, is the «French Way».

The moon at dawn is a silent witness of
our departure, the day begins

The stages

The road is divided into stages. The Guides usually recommend specific stages that coincide with the cities with the largest population, since they are the ones with more accommodation to choose from and more services. This is only a suggestion, because in small towns we can also find good accommodation and basic services. We are free to decide the stages, and we will do it according to our strengths.

Each day begins at the place where the night has passed (hostel, refuge, hotel) and ends at the place of destination. It is possible, but not advisable, to improvise where we are going to spend the night. A twenty something can improvise, and sleep in the open if all the accommodations are full, but for the other people it is advisable to plan well the following days, especially the accommodations.

The plan must have some flexibility and consider the physical state which we are in. If we have some type of severe muscle pain it is better not to start the day and instead rest and continue the next day. In all the towns there is usually a pharmacy where they will help us and in many cities there are physiotherapists.

The days start at dawn. It is good to leave when the day clears to arrive without stress at the destination before noon, thus avoiding the hours of greatest heat from the sun. For this reason, on days when there is a forecast of cloudy skies, it is possible to postpone the departure time a little.

The road meanders up the mountain,
where storm clouds are waiting

Types of roads

The Camino is not a uniform route. Some sections are formed by wide rural roads where the tractors pass comfortably, others by narrow paths and still others by steep paths between bushes. There are flat stretches where you can see the next town located five kilometers away, and other sections are so steep that we have to help ourselves with a cane to climb, so as not to slip and fall. A few sections circulate on the roadside are even paved, while others are a stony road where you have to be careful not to twist your ankle.

We will move along dusty dry roads, and also through other roads so muddy that we will have to jump from stone to stone. There are sections where the smell of the herbs impregnates us with health, and other sections where the smell of the pig and cows farms makes us accelerate the pace to leave behind the pestilence. We will find all these types of roads.

You have to be prepared with strong and comfortable footwear that hold your feet well and also protects against both the cold of the morning and the heat of midday.

It is important to note that there are no stretches of climbing or mountaineering and therefore « mountain boots » are not necessary. Select comfortable and very durable footwear for walking.

2. Make the decision (6 months before)

Pilgrims and tourists can appreciate the beauty
reflected in delicate works of art

The reason

Pilgrims, that is, people who do it for a religious reason, like winning the Jubilee or penance, know well what their purpose is.

On the other hand, tourists, with many nuances, usually want to know places, people, meals, do some physical exercise, stay a few days with the couple, etc. and some say reasons for personal improvement.

I will assume that you are not a fool who sets out to cover 800 km. (500 miles) in a blind adventure. Therefore, identifying the true motivation is important, very important.

People having crossed the barrier of 60 like me have the possibility of doing things that before the work and the infinite obligations have not allowed. Now that the working life is over, we have the opportunity to do things, even crazy things, that if health permits, nobody will prevent us.

In summary, if you are a urbanite who sits all day in an office, it is logical that you want to walk; if you work in an unhealthy office, you want to be able to breathe clean air; if you have been waiting all day for clients and colleagues, now you want to enjoy the solitude; if you have been forced to achieve goals, you want to do something where the end is not a goal; and finally, if you have spent too little time with your wife and friends, now you can recover part of those lost moments. You can say goodbye to all that for a few days and go to the Camino, with a thousand reasons.

The high mountains are inhabited by giants who observe our step with hidden curiosity

Which route to choose

Now that you identified your motivation, are ready to choose your route. I suggest, that you tell your friends, and yourself, that you are not going to do « El Camino », that is, to walk the almost 800 km. They cross Spain almost from end to end, and such a goal is too large. Instead, think that you will make « some days » of the Camino. The nuance is important, because if for example you start at Roncesvalles you can leave it at any time without it being a failure. You just went to do « some days » and you've done them. Also, if you raise it in this way you leave the door open to continue another time in the place you left it. This way of proceeding is common for people who live in Spain and can do ten or twelve days a year, leave it and return the following year. For visitors this is somewhat more expensive, and why they attempt the Camino in one go.

If we do not take Santiago de Compostela as a goal, we can better enjoy each stage, take breaks if there is bad weather or we feel like visiting the city, and if we finally arrive in Santiago, it will have been without stress and with less suffering.

As a simple point of reference, the author made a four-year plan. In the first year was Roncesvalles to Pamplona, which is only 45 km. The second was two stages, first from Pamplona to Logroño before the summer, about 100 km., and later from Logroño to Burgos, 125 km., after the summer. The third year went from Burgos to Ponferrada, 290 km, and the fourth from Ponferrada to Santiago de Compostela, another 220 km. No rush or hassles, and calmly visiting the cathedrals and cities. We will discuss planning in more detail later in the book.

The way offers surprises that no guide can anticipate

Books and guides

The books and guides help us plan the general route first, and then the detail. On the internet there is a lot of information, you can also download a file on the mobile that shows on Google Earth in detail the Camino route at http: //www.elcaminosantiago.com

How is the road

You have to take good note of the kilometers for each day, where the towns are, and the profile of the road. Knowing what the day will hold is important to distribute the challenges and plan the stops accordingly.

What to see or visit

The more information you have about hermitages, bridges, valleys, rivers, mountains, stories and legends, the more you will enjoy the day.

Where to eat

In the guides and on the internet there is information about the villages, towns or cities where you can stop to eat. The food is usually good and plentiful.

Where to stay

It is usual to make a reservation by phone a week or two in advance, and it is essential to confirm the reservation the day before. The reservation portals do not include hostels, for those you have to consult the aforementioned website or Google Maps.

What is life? A frenzy
What is life? An illusion,
a shadow, a fiction,
and the greatest good is small;
that all life is a dream,
and dreams, dreams are.

    Calderón de la Barca
    Poet

Alone or accompanied

During the Camino (French Way) we will not have a feeling of loneliness, even though if we look back and forth, we will not see anyone. If we stop at any point, before ten or fifteen minutes, someone will soon pass. So we can do the Camino alone without problems because it is not a lonely place.

Doing it accompanied by another person has many advantages, especially if it is our partner. In the first place that means that both have good health and similar tastes, so the Camino will provide shared experiences. Some months before do the rehearsals together, and see the pace at which each one can go, and if the one that would go a little faster can load more weight in the backpack and slow down. It is not difficult for two people to organize to walk together. Luckily there is a lot of accommodation available with rooms for two people, which usually guarantees better rest.

On the other hand, being accompanied by more than one person seems quite complicated. There will always be one who wants to go fast like a hare, another who despite his progress moves at a snail's pace, and a third who must balance between them. In addition, they soon discover that the width of the road in many sections allows only two people to advance side by side, but does not have width for three or more. No matter how much harmony there is between them, the group ends up disintegrating shortly after leaving.

Think about your motivation and be cautious about being more than two people, so you don't have unneeded stress.

Along the way you can choose between all types of accommodation, from the simplest to the luxurious.

Budget

Most bars, restaurants and many accommodations have bad telecoms coverage and do not accept cards. For this reason you have to carry cash, as often there are no ATMs in all the towns, it is convenient to carry the cash for three or four days, which is not a high sum (prepayment is not usual except in hotels).

The prices, from the first town to the last are very similar, more or less as follows:
- Menu for lunch or dinner: 10 euros.
- Snack and breakfast or snack drink: 5 euros.
- Bottle of 500 cc of water (fresh!): 1 euro (2 per day)
- Accommodation: in albergues 12 euros per bunk, in a hostel or hotel: 50 euros a double room.

The total per person, staying in hostels, is about 60 euros per day. Assuming 35 days of walking plus 5 days unplanned stops, the total is about 2,500 euros. For a couple it is double.

Purchasing a backpack, footwear, etc. should be added as an expense, even though for the most part they will return home with us. Although sometimes it is possible to wash clothes for free, sometimes we must go to laundries (10 euros per day). Most laundries are open 24 hours. In addition, in each case it will be necessary to pay for trips from home to the point of departure and return from Santiago de Compostela or mid-way to home. As disbursements we can add the cost of taking the suitcase from one accommodation to another (120 euros for the 35 stages with the post service Correos). Adding some visits to museums, incidentals and whims you have to budget approximately 3,000 euros per head.

We all know how to walk, to do it many days requires determination, courage and preparation

In summary: yes or no

You must know that « want is power » is silly. Sometimes we want to do things that we can no longer do. Let's try a simple test to know what you want. Choose one answer:

    1. Field or city?

    2. Sitting or walking?

    3. Breakfast at 7 or 10?

If you have answered the field, walk and at 7, doing the Camino you will enjoy ecstasy.

Now let's see if you can. Answer Yes or No:

    4. Do you ever go to the gym or pool?

    5. Do you have heart problems?

    6. Do you have family responsibilities?

If you answered Yes, No, No, go ahead.

Otherwise, if you do not do anything physical, have heart problems, or have to take care of a relative even though you want to, at the moment you cannot.

However, as the will moves mountains, do not abandon your dream. Calmly, you can start making longer and longer walks, 1, 3, 5, 15, 25 kilometers under medical supervision, progressing little by little, and then look for a gap in your family obligations to do some days of the Camino.

3. Planning
(3 months before)

Everything seems to point the way,
or maybe it's just an illusion

Starting point

Walkers are free to choose the starting point they want. If your goal is to reach Santiago de Compostela, as a pilgrim, or because as a tourist you want to receive the «Compostela», yes or yes, you should look at the days available. Calculate the days that will do at a rate of about 20 km. per day, add a day of break every 5 or 6 days, and you will find the town or city that will be your starting point. Now you only have to plan how you will arrive the day before starting (car, train, bus).

Otherwise, if you are not a pilgrim and therefore arriving in Santiago is not essential, or as a tourist you do not think it so important to get the « Compostela » ... my personal suggestion would be to start in Roncesvalles.

Roncesvalles is the first Spanish town on the French Way. It is at the top of the Pyrenees, and the journey to Pamplona is basically downhill (with some unavoidable slopes). Roncesvalles is a good place to start because the stages from there go between forests, which protect you from the sun and excessive heat, enemies of the walker. To get to Roncesvalles, take a bus from Pamplona or a taxi (shared is cheaper) and in an hour you will reach Roncesvalles.

The «French Way» begins formally in Saint Jean Pied De Port, but starting there has two problems. The first is the difficulty finding transportation, and second and most importantly, you start at 180 meters so you have to climb up to 1,426 meters. To do that on the first day is brutal, so I do not recommend it.

The last snows in the peaks of the mountains indicate that the roads are already passable

The start date

Doing the Camino one Thursday is the same as one Saturday, August as March.

It is not a good idea to do the Camino in July or August, as it is very hot in the fields. Also, everything is much more expensive, overcrowded and the worst service. Let's leave those months for the unfortunate students and workers who have no choice but to stick with the heat, the prices and the queues in the restaurants.

It is also not a good idea to do it in the coldest months, which are usually December, January and February. The days are shorter, the roads are usually muddy, and there is a risk that a snowfall will surprise us. Also in those months many accommodations and restaurants are closed.

So, since we can choose, we will do the Camino in March, April, May, June, September, October or November.

In those months we will meet many people from around the world who come well prepared and informed.

Once the date is decided, we must be flexible, as a storm may delay us a couple of days, or perhaps we will not go through Burgos or León like an arrow without seeing its cathedrals and museums.

The sunset is time for meditation and
preparation for the next stage

Plan the stages

In the duration of the next stage we must take into account the orography, especially the unevenness of the road, the populations where we can stay, and the expected weather.

The typical profile of a stage is a flat road with some undulations of the terrain. It is not surprising that there are some steep slopes, but nothing that can not be overcome with patience. The solution to a day that has steep slopes and strong climbs is to go a little slower, and take some extra time. The real danger is that we reach the noon hour (between 13 and 14 hours) far from our destination or any town. In full sun, after a long day, walking causes a lot of fatigue, so we must plan to achieve our destination before noon.

Each day the distance to be traveled is calculated based on the speed at which we can move forward, taking into account the slope of the road. A normal day should be about 20 kilometers. We can go down to 15 km. if the slope is pronounced, we are going to stop along the road in some special place, we want to have a day of rest, or because it coincides with an important city. We can plan something more than 20 kilometers, but it is not a good idea to stretch to 25. The days are marked by towns, in general every 5 kilometers we will find a place to rest and regain strength.

Remember that the Camino is not a journey through the desert. In case of need it is always possible to take a taxi to our destination.

The accommodation is essential to rest well at night,
and be ready for the next day

Accommodations

With few exceptions all the accommodations are excellent: clean, quiet and friendly with friendly staff. It is mostly like that, usually. That does not mean that there are not some hostels (very few) of hippy aesthetics that are simply crappy with a nest of diverse critters.

In hotels, hostels and other accommodations it is customary to book the room by telephone one or two weeks before, but it is essential to confirm it the day before. Without confirmation there is no room.

We all need to rest well at night, and it is better not to skimp on this expense. The prices of nice rooms for two people with bathroom is usually 50 euros / night; very reasonable. Prices will vary depending on how close or far the hotel is to the Camino, whether it includes breakfast or not.

The specific accommodations for the Camino walkers are called « albergue », they do not permit stays of more than one night, except for justified cause (injury), and at 8 in the morning guests must all leave. Some hostels, very few, include a cafeteria where you can have breakfast but at 7 in the morning they do not usually have fresh bread of the day. It becomes a task of the previous afternoon to find out where we can have breakfast before starting the next day to avoid the risk of starting on an empty stomach.

Hotel search internet portals do not usually include the « albergues », so you must go to websites on the Camino or Google Maps to discover the complete list of available accommodations.

4. Preparations
(1 month before)

The sculptures located in singular places
they break the monotony of long journeys

Test routes

Even if you do some physical exercise to stay healthy, you need to rehearse well before you start the Camino. A half an hour of elliptical and a few laps in the pool is not the same as walking for six or seven hours. The intensity of the effort is different, as are the muscles that are used.

A normal stage of the Camino is between 20 and 25 kilometers. Thus at a rate of 4 kilometers an hour a day is about 6 hours, plus stops for breaks.

You can now see the wisdom of preparation, nobody cannot just start walking for 6 hours per day. Starting a month before, the trials should be of a progressive intensity. Start with a few kilometers and increase them as we see how we finish the day. Start with one or two walks per week, and increase the frequency as we see that we recover.

The choice of where to rehearse should include varying terrain, with some slopes and their corresponding descents. Avoid completely flat places such as boardwalks.

The purpose of the rehearsals is to improve our walking form as well as to try on the footwear, cap, and other clothing, as well as to choose the right backpack.

You will be ready when you can do three days in a row of 20 kilometers, carrying water, some food, and a light backpack, without finishing exhausted.

Neither the rain, the wind or the incessant sun
are obstacles for walkers

Clothing and footwear

Even in the best time of the year, along the Camino you will cross sunny and hot deserts, and walk through the fog of a cold and windy morning. The clothing should be appropriate for such changing environments. You also have to carry more than one change of clothes, for after the daily shower.

If you do not want to spend a few days suffering in overwhelming heat and deadly cold on other days, you need clothes that can be adapted to the weather in the day.

The solution is to take a backpack and a small suitcase with wheels (trolley). In the backpack you can carry a basic change in case we are surprised by a storm and get wet, next to a light raincoat or poncho. The rest of the clothes remain in the trolley, which, as we will explain later, the post office will forward to our next accommodation.

Footwear must be appropriate for dirt roads. It is not necessary to wear mountain boots, nor is it appropriate to wear moccasin shoes. Better choices are lightweight but sturdy shoes for hot days and leather boots for the days that dawn colder. Remember that « snakes do not bite those who wear boots ».

It is essential to take flip flops. When you reach your destination remove your shoes or boots, and let your feet breathe with simple flip flops ... until the next day.

We must always walk carefully,
as a false step can send us back home

Backpack and cane

The rehearsal days should have helped us to select what we have to carry in the backpack. It is important that the backpack is light, with a side mesh where you can have a bottle of water handy. The wallet, mobile, pills, keys and kleenex in the pockets of the trousers.

Mandatory items for each day for the backpack: 500 cm3 (1/2 litre) bottle of water, sandwich or nuts, a buff or scarf to wear in the first hour and then stow it, hat, sunglasses, raincoat and a complete change of clothes, including trousers. Take also a very basic first aid kit, with some band-aid and little else. Very useful are « macaroni » bandages, similar to strips but cylindrical for the toes.

It is optional to bring sun cream, and also a light sweater and gloves in case the day changes. Do not carry books or guides in your backpack, read them before you start the day and store them in your trolley.

A long walking stick rather than a short cane is important. Rare will be the day you do not use it, either to support you on a steep climb or to make sure you are steady on a slippery slope. It also prevents the hands from swelling after hours of walking, since you keep them at the height of the heart. Perhaps the most appropriate design is one of wood with a metal tip, that can be stuck in the mud, and one that is light. There are aluminum poles, but on the Camino they are seldom seen; wooden ones are better.

The bell towers point to a village,
a town or a city for rest

Luggage

Taking as a principle that we do not want to suffer unnecessarily, it is necessary to prepare the essential luggage well. It will be divided in two: daily needs that we will carry in the backpack, and the rest in the suitcase or trolley that Correos will take for us every day from one accommodation to another.

Backpack

You must always carry with you the documentation, credit card, health insurance card, cash, house keys, hat, mobile phone, sunglasses and cane. Some of these ítems, plus your Pilgrim's credentials, will go in a sealed plastic bag. It is also essential to bring a water bottle, some food (cookies or nuts), buff or scarf, bandages, a small knife, the medication that you must take during the day, plus kleenex. Optional but recommended ítems are: camera, flip flops, a full change of clothes and a raincoat, all according to the weather forecast.

Suitcase-trolley

Your remaining gear, not essential for the day, will stay in the trolley. You will take the usual ítems for a trip, that is, at least one change of clothes, a well-stocked kit especially for mosquito bites and muscle relaxant ointment, medication for two weeks, sun cream, hair dryer, towel, plus kleenex, soap shower and shampoo. Also include the shaving accessories you need. You have to place a transparent plastic envelope tied with a ribbon to the handle of the suitcase where you will insert the Correos (Spanish Post Office) form, that tells you where they should take your suitcase.

Photography enthusiasts can find endless opportunities for great photos

Mobile and camera

For photography enthusiasts this is an opportunity to take spectacular images throughout each day; from a sunrise that is reflected in a lake, following the silhouette of a tree that can be guessed among the morning mists, some butterflies, a belfry with its storks, the gloom of a hermitage, and so on. You should look for powerful but light photography equipment, because you will have to carry it around for six hours every day. A note of caution: limit the taking of pictures so it does not delays you, because the time runs and the sun is getting higher and warmer.

For the non-enthusiast we have two options. One is to use the camera of the mobile, and another is to look for a small digital camera. These will to capture the moments of where we were, nice features of that town and so on because memory is not what it was. These souvenir photos will also jog our memory of details that do not appear in the photos when we show them to friends and family. Perhaps we will regret some picture we did not take, but at least we did not take it four times. Remember that there are two kinds of photos: the kind that you have backed-up and the kind you haven't lost yet.

We have examined what we should take, let's see what is best left behind. At the top of this list are radios or music helmets. The best sounds will be found at each step we take. You may not know what kind of bird is singing, but surely it is one you will not hear when you return home.

Places, dates, moments, and emotions
leave their mark on the Pilgrim's Credential

Pilgrim's Credential

People who arrive in Santiago de Compostela receive a certificate called « Compostela » in the Pilgrim's Office, if they prove that they have made at least the last one hundred kilometers on foot, or two hundred by bicycle.

To prove we have made the journey there is the «Pilgrim Credential». It has several formats but the most common one is an extendable sheet that folds like an accordion.

Churches, hermitages, bars, restaurants, and lodgings will add their seal to the document and next to the stamp they will record the date. It is advisable to obtain a seal at least a couple of times a day, and it is useful both to prove the lego of the trip we have just done, and so that later we ourselves can better remember where we were and the dates.

The credential costs a few euros, and it is not available in all locations or at all hours. Plan ahead, using the internet for the Pilgrim Office schedule of the city where you are going to start, to obtain a credential before the first day.

Also, a new credential will be needed when the previous one is full of stamps. Again a reminder that they do not sell credentials in all places, but they are available in the Pilgrim Offices of Roncesvalles, Burgos, León and Ponferrada, during their opening hours.

Not everyone who starts the Camino concludes it,
do not be one of them.

Take care

Every year several people die while they are doing in Camino. The main causes are falls, traffic accidents, and heart attacks.

It is easy to stumble and even fall by doing so many kilometers a day, usually with no consequences. Still, we must take extreme precautions and look where we tread. Dislocating an ankle may be the end of the adventure. The serious, and sometimes deadly, falls occur in gullies. You can count on the fingers of one hand the few places where the walkers have to advance in single file due to lack of space. In mountainous areas; however, there is always a small risk of getting lost, leaving the road and falling down a ravine. Going in company decreases the risk of getting lost. When in doubt, going back is a good idea.

The traffic accidents occur in those places where the Camino crosses a road, sometimes in the rain or fog. We have to think that with the backpack we move slower than normal, and above all, we do not have any priority when crossing the road.

Heart attacks, whether during the day or upon arrival at the accommodation, are caused by overexertion. If the day has been planned well, it should not happen. However, it is possible that unforeseen events arise for which then require extra effort to reach the next accommodation. In this case it is better to take a long break, sit down, and end the day later in the afternoon. Some will call a taxi to take us to the accommodation; do this if completing the day's walk will be too much. As a last option you can call 112, the European Union emergency number.

"Bedbugs, protagonists of the Camino de Santiago" La Razón 10/22/2023. It is not alarming, but according to the managers of several albergue, cases do occur. These insects spread in backpacks and their public transportation. Tips: 1. Do not leave backpacks on the ground when making stops during the day. 2. Check the folds of the bed mattress. 3. Notify the albergue staff if you detect bedbugs.

Papilloma. It is a virus that causes warts on the soles of the feet. It is not serious but requires medical treatment. It is spread if there is an injury to the feet and if one steps on wet surfaces barefoot. Albergues showers are very frequented places where it is possible to get infected. Tip: Wear flip flops in the showers.

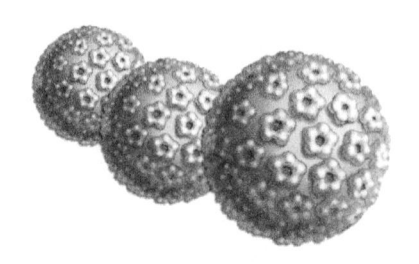

5. Running
(1 day before)

Singular pillory, serene witness of times
distant, present and future

The first day

We try to remember how and when the idea of doing the Camino began and we are no longer sure how it came to our head. It does not matter, we are ready and determined.

Day D-1 has arrived, you are in the accommodation where tomorrow you will start the road. It is time for a last moment of reflection before starting the Camino; nobody forces you to start as soon as nobody will force you to continue.

The most surprising thing for me is not so much the large number of people who start the Camino as the fact that the vast majority finish it.

At dinner time you will see people, young and old, Spaniards and foreigners, some who are about to start and others, with flip-flops, no doubt have been walking for several days. At this time and in this place all here are doing the same.

At dinner you will discover that the atmosphere is a strange complicity, almost even of camaraderie between people who do not know each other, many who do not speak the same language, and almost certainly they will not meet again at a table.

From now on, breakfasts, lunches and dinners will be more sober than copious. It is not an obligation of the doctor, but nobody climbs a hill with a heavy stomach so plan for very light meals.

The yellow arrows, in markers, soil or walls,
indicate the direction to follow

Some things to do

Every day, in the afternoon, you must prepare well for the following day:

- Call the next accommodation by phone to confirm the reservation. This is essential! An unconfirmed reservation is a voided reservation.

- Find the breakfast place for the next morning. You need to find a bar open at 7 in the morning, or better yet a bakery because they will make you a sandwich with bread of the day. Finding such a place is not easy.

- Check the weather forecast: sun, rain, and expected daytime temperatures for tomorrow in the area. When you get up in the morning you will check that there are no changes.

- Review tomorrow's route, distances, places to rest or eat, and places of interest to visit.

- Determine the exact location of your next accommodation, so as not to go searching the town when you arrive as generally you will be very tired.

- Repack the backpack and suitcase, and change the label to the address of the next accommodation.

- Buy the pilgrim's credential if you do not have one. You have to be prepared with a credential before you depart.

- Find the exit route of the city, which is neither obvious nor easy in large cities.

- Eat and go to sleep early. Tomorrow you have to get up early, wake up at 6:30 to leave at 7:00

6. The stages

Colors and ruins welcome
the attentive visitor

A personal experience

What follows next are a few comments, one page per day, based on my personal experience. They are not a precise guide because they do not detail kilometers, terrain, cities or places. They offer the value of a personal experience, and of what, as a summary I can remember.

Each person will have different experiences in the same place, as a result of their training, the climate of that moment, or who they find there, their health, or any contingencies that may happen. It is important to plan each day, but also to welcome the surprises of the thousands of factors that we cannot control. We may find a dead hare by the road, a fisherman who was not there yesterday, a popular party that is held once a year, or a mass gathering for the dead. We will be surprised by tiny Asian women covered from head to toe in the sun, who march slowly but arrive at the end of each day.

The ornithologist will enjoy the varied types of birds that he will find, the architect will enjoy the columns and lintels, the urbanites enjoying the sun, the wind, the rains, rivers, lightning and storms.

If we go with the mind and the senses fully awake we can have experiences that no guide book collects. How could a book describe the smell of the fields after the rain? Or the swaying of the stalks of grain in the golden fields, the terrible image of a centennial oak broken by lightning, or the taste of a « pincho de tortilla » with bread, in a bustling village bar. It is necessary to let the soul breathe, feel, laugh and cry in this long and exciting journey.

Just follow the signs

Some things that happen

1. Badges, pins and scallops. It is evident that a person with a backpack on the Camino de Santiago route is there for that sole purpose. We must decide if we are going to carry the backpack with badges, pins or a scallop. A logical approach is for pilgrims to take scallops, while the rest of the people carry badges or pins as a souvenir.

2. Time of departure. You have to get up early each day and start the journey as soon as it is light, to try to reach your destination accommodation shortly before noon, avoiding the hottest hours. Each day's journey will be more than 20 km, and you cannot run or accelerate the pace, so the only option is to start early, and then move slowly and with few pauses.

3. The afternoon is free. If you have complied with your schedule, you will arrive at noon at the accommodation. Wash, eat, and take the whole afternoon to rest or visit the place. Pilgrims have the opportunity to attend mass, except in small villages. Now it's time to replace boots with flip-flops - you'll see many people in flip-flops - so your feet are fresh for the next day.

4. Leave if you do not like it. If you are not comfortable doing the Camino it is illogical to complain, go away. There is no reason to complain about the small hardships of the road when at any moment you can leave. The grumpy discover that on the road they are a « rare bird ». If you do not like the Camino do not give explanations, ask for a taxi at any bar, and in half an hour you will be at the hotel and from there to your home.

The sturdy trees seem to protect
the path of any danger

5. Sick. If you feel bad, use common sense and your experience. If you are in your accommodation, it is best not to start the day, change the plan and take a day off; consult the doctor if it is serious. Your companion will understand. If you are in a town, it is best to take a long break, as long as necessary, and leave when you are much better, not a little better. If you are in the middle of fields, look for some shade where you can sit down, drink water and eat something. Be patient if you are just waiting for someone to come along the way who can help. Telephone coverage is spotty, so you may not be able to call 112; in this case do not stay alone.

6. Bugs and pests. The road, especially the surroundings, is full of bugs so it is better not to sit or lie on the ground. Some are annoying, like ants. Others are very annoying, like flies and spiders, and some can give you slight problems, such as ticks, bugs, mosquitoes, wasps. Still others are disgusting and more troublesome like snakes. Even if you do not see them, they are there. Do not get too far off the road or trail, wear good shoes and do not lie on the grass. Enjoy the other varieties of bugs: butterflies, mantis, slugs, snails, salamanders, grasshoppers, beetles, ladybugs, bees, dragonflies, etc. that will accompany you fleetingly.

7. Photos. Plan how and where you are going to store the photos you are taking. Be mindful of the capacity limit of the memory of your mobile phone or camera. Every two or three days back up the photos to a safe place. Test the back up before leaving.

8. Stretching. It is recommended at the end of the day to lighten the legs. The other walkers can show you how to do it. Five minutes is all that is required.

7. The Frech Camino

Villages, towns, cities, hermitages,
churches, cathedrals form the way

Distances km.

1. Roncesvalles - Burguete 3,0
2. Burguete - Zubiri 19,0
3. Zubiri - Pamplona 21,0
4. Pamplona - Puente la Reina 24,0
5. Puente la Reina - Estella 22,0
6. Estella - Los Arcos 22,0
7. Los Arcos - Viana 19,0
8. Viana - Logroño 10,0
9. Logroño - Nájera 30,0
10. Nájera - Santo Domingo de la Calzada 21,0
11. Sto. Domingo de la Calzada - Belorado 23,0
12. Belorado - Agés 28,0
13. Agés - Burgos 23,0
14. Burgos - Hontanas 32,0
15. Hontanas - Boadilla del Camino 29,0
16. Boadilla - Carrión de los Condes 25,0
17. Carrión de los Condes - Terradillos 27,0
18. Terradillos - El Burgo Ranero 31,0
19. El Burgo - Mansilla de las Mulas 19,0
20. Mansilla de las Mulas - León 19,0
21. León - San Martín del Camino 27,0
22. San Martín del Camino - Astorga 25,0
23. Astorga - Rabanal del Camino 21,0
24. Rabanal del Camino - El Acebo 18,0
25. El Acebo - Ponferrada 16,0
26. Ponferrada - Villafranca del Bierzo 25,0
27. Villafranca del Bierzo - Las Herrerías 21,0
28. Las Herrerías - O Cebreiro 9,0
29. O Cebreiro - Triacastela 22,0
30. Triacastela - Sarria 25,0
31. Sarria - Portomarín 23,0
32. Portomarín - Palas de Rei 25,0
33. Palas de Rei - A Fraga Alta 23,0
34. A Fraga Alta - O Pedrouzo 26,0
35. O Pedrouzo - Santiago de Compostela 21,0

Like in a huge museum, the art of
the churches come out to meet us

Accommodations visited

Only as a mere comment for the reader of this book, the accommodations that have been visited are indicated below. All have double rooms, most with a bathroom, and are priced between € 40 and € 60 per night, breakfast not included.

The quality of all the accommodations on the Camino is very good. It is not intended to offer here a list of the best at each place, only to provide a positive first-hand reference based on the observed cleanliness and the quality of the facilities.

1. Burguete
    Hostal Burguete Tel. 948 760 005
2. Zubiri
    Hostal Gau Txori Tel. 948 304 076
3. Pamplona
    Hotel Burlada Tel 948 131 300
4. Puente la Reina
    Hostal Plaza Tel. 948 340 145
5. Estella
    Camping Iratxe Tel. 948 555 555
6. Los Arcos
    Hostal Ezequiel Tel. 948 640 107
7. Viana
    Hotel Palacio Pujadas Tel. 948 646 464
8. Logroño
    NH Logroño Tel. 941 519 270
9. Nájera
    Albergue Puerta de Nájera Tel. 941 362 231
10. Santo Domingo de la Calzada
    Parador de Sto. Domingo Tel. 941 341 150

A centenary oak looks attentive ly
at the slow progress of walkers

11. Belorado
    Hotel Jacobeo Tel. 947 580 010
12. Agés
    Albergue San Rafael Tel. 947 430 392
13. Burgos
    Hotel Silken Gran Teatro Tel. 947 253 900
14. Hontanas
    Albergue Juan de Yepes Tel. 638 938 546
15. Boadilla del Camino
    Hotel Rural En el Camino Tel 979 810 999
16. Carrión de los Condes
    Hostal Santiago Tel. 979 881 052
17. Terradillos de los Templarios
    Albergue los Templarios Tel. 667 252 279
18. El Burgo Ranero
    Hotel Rural Piedras Blancas Tel. 987 330 094
19. Mansilla de las Mulas
    Alberguería del Camino Tel. 987 311 193
20. León
    Exe Campus San Mamés Tel. 987 34 70 33
21. San Martín del Camino
    Albergue Santa Ana Tel. 654 111 509
22. Astorga
    Via de la Plata Spa Tel. 987 619 000
23. Rabanal del Camino
    Albergue Ntra.Sra. del Pilar Tel. 616 089 942
24. El Acebo
    La Casa del Peregrino Tel. 987 057 793
25. Ponferrada
    Hotel Novo
26. Villafranca del Bierzo
    Hostal Burbia Tel. 987 542 667
27. Las Herrerías
    Casa Polín Tel. 987 543 039
28. O Cebreiro
    Casa Rural Venta Celta Tel. 667 553 006

In the heights the fog merges with the clouds

29. Triacastela
    Complexo Xacobeo Tel. 982 548 037
30. Sarria
    Hotel Mar de Plata Tel. 982 530 724
31. Portomarín
    Pensión Pérez Tel. 615 996 868
32. Palas de Rei
    Pensión Barcelona Tel. 982 374 114
33. A Fraga Alta
    Albergue Santiago Tel. 981 50 17 11
34. O Pedrouzo
    Pensión Residencial Platas Tel . 981 511 378
35. Santiago de Compostela
    Hospedería San Martín Pinario T. 981 560 282

The poster announcing the miles to go does not
impress the people who start, but it should.

Stage 1. Roncesvalles - Burguete

We decided to start our Camino with this mini-stage of about 3 km. to serve as mental and physical preparation. We bought the pilgrim credential and start calmly with a shorter stage that same day.

We had arrived in Pamplona by train mid-morning and then we took a bus in the afternoon to Roncesvalles. There are only two bus departures a day from Pamplona: morning or afternoon. The morning bus is designed for people to spend the night in the hostel in Pamplona and start in Roncesvalles the next morning; the afternoon bus is designed for those who wish to spend the night in the hostel in Roncesvalles and start the day the following day. In our case, we took the afternoon bus and after an hour of travel we arrived in Roncesvalles, bought the credential in the Pilgrim's Office and without waiting for the sun to set we walked to the first town, Burguete. We are not the only ones who have that idea.

The trip to Burguete is 3 kilometers on a flat, wide road, almost in a straight line crossing fields with grazing cows and a forest with the first milestones of the Camino. The stage is done in a half hour. We take our first photos. A stone cross marks the arrival at Burguete. Curious about the town, we walk down the sidewalks and down to an irrigation canal. We look for our accommodation, a place to dine and a place to have breakfast tomorrow.

We have not yet discovered that Correos can take the suitcases of pilgrims to their next accommodation, so we carry our backpacks loaded with everything.

The steep slope at the exit of Lintzoain
begins to test the will of the walkers.

Stage 2. Burguete - Zubiri

In the morning, when we wake up and look through the window of the room, we see several people with backpacks going through the main street of Burguete. It was evident that we will not be among the first. We will try not to be the last.

We have a little less than 20 kilometers ahead of us when we have breakfast and we start up. A large yellow arrow on the asphalt of the main street shows us the way to go, plus we can follow the other people who start the day like us. Each at his own pace and in silence.

The day begins in descent, we cross the bridge over a river, but soon a steep slope arrives. Up and down to the village of Espinal, where we can enter a bar to seal the credential. It is a good place to buy a wooden cane if you do not already have one.

After two hours, we have traveled about 10 km. and we arrive at Lintzoain, which is four houses. At the exit we expect a rise of 45° slope, but is not slippery because the ground is cement. At each step we give ourselves encouragement thinking that it takes less to finish the steep street.

We continue the ascent to Erro in continuous ups and downs that prevent a uniform pace. At the top of Erro there is a bar-trailer where we take advantage of a cold drink. There are less than 4 km. until Zubiri, which is done quickly because it is downhill. We cross the bridge of La Rabia, it is 1 pm in the afternoon, and we will find our accommodation.

Peaceful day, among forests, ideal for walking
enjoying the charms of the landscape.

Stage 3. Zubiri - Pamplona

We have about 20 km planned for today. We left Zubiri, going back across the bridge of La Rabia in the opposite direction. We will follow the course of the river Arga between forests, and we will descend from 525 meters of altitude to 420 meters in the city of Pamplona.

Less than a kilometer away starts a steep descent on wooden steps awaits us, where we begin to discover the usefulness of the cane. Then a cobbled road where you have to be wary of each step. All this forces us to go slowly, and with caution. The milestones of the Camino tell us that we are on the right path.

We decided not to take many photos, which we will later regret. We did take a picture of a beautiful fountain with a sign « Water not drinkable », and later we passed a house guarded by geese that seem aggressive, so a couple of photos and we are on our way.

Halfway through the day, in a picnic area at the exit of Irotz, we are offered three options to go to Pamplona. The choice is complicated, but since we are not tired at all, we decided to take the road of Burlada, shorter although it is described as having a steep rise, which we soon discovered was accurate.

Thus, almost without realizing it, we arrived at the first city on the route. At least we can already say that we made the Camino de Santiago from Ronvesvalles to Pamplona. Although we already knew the city from the Sanfermines, we take a day off to see it more calmly.

In the Alto del Perdón a sculpture welcomes us and is a place to rest and eat

Stage 4. Pamplona - Puente la Reina

In summary this day has about 12 km. up to Alto del Perdón and then another 12 km. down to Puente la Reina.

Since we are rested after one full day in Pamplona, and today is long, we decided to leave shortly before dawn and we see the sunrise over the mountains. We cross next to a large pool of water and at that moment we are surprised by a flock of birds in perfect formation moving north. All priceless for an urbanite.

After two hours on the road, we arrived at Zariquiegui where an exquisite omelette skewer and a visit to the bathroom set us up to continue. We see modern windmills in what we suppose to be the Alto del Perdón. It is a steep climb surrounded by scrubland, but it does not bother us because the early sun is not hot and it is a north slope. Slowly, step by step, we reach the top. We discovered a sculpture that shows a set of pilgrims, photos and more photos. A group of Brazilians arrive, then another of Canadians, each with his flag in his backpack, and next some Asians but we cannot tell from which country. There is a small traveling bar that we do not use.

We start our descent on a path of loose stones, frequently using the cane to avoid falling on our backside. There are small lilac flowers of saffron; beautiful. We arrive in Muruzabal after a climb and enter into a large square with a very unique church facade. We cross into Puente la Reina and help an Asian couple find their accommodation. Next we go directly to our accommodation and then find a restaurant that is open. We are fortunate to have arrived during the « roasted pepper week », with fair days and parties.

A careful world map surprises the walker
in a field at the exit of Cirauqui

Stage 5. Puente la Reina - Estella

The profile of our stage for today warns us to expect a climb shortly after leaving Puente la Reina. It is much steeper than expected. An almost vertical dirt road puts us to the test. Calm, a lot of calm, with pauses when necessary. If this is a medieval route it is clear that the cavalries climbed here, but it is impassible by carts. The one that has positive energy to spare shares it with the companion, because either we arrive together or we go back home.

The day introduces us to the town of Cirauqui, about 8 km. from Puente la Reina. It is of noble bearing, well conserved and located on a hill. We climb slowly and enter under a medieval door, seal the credential in the door of the church, take some photos. We continue on what we are told is an authentic Roman road, 2nd century, followed by a stretch of large stones in steep descent to a bridge. A little further on we will cross another bridge, this one under the Salado (Salty) river, of dubious reputation.

About 5 km. from Cirauqui is Lorca, and another 5 km. is Villatuerta, and 5 km more is Estella, so we can decide where to make stops according to our mood. Lorca is a small town with an interesting church at the entrance.

A long descent takes us to Villatuerta (One-eye town), an ugly name for a beautiful place. There is a beautiful bridge over the Irantzu river, and steep streets or so it seems.

The town of Estella, after crossing the river Ega, is a stone's throw away.

Villamayor de Monjardín, church of San Andrés, the cross and the sword a few meters away

Stage 6. Estella - Los Arcos

The previous afternoon in Estella we leisurely visited Irache Wineries, with the vineyard, a highly recommended visit. The nearby Monastery of Santa Maria de Irache is also very interesting. Irache camping, a place where they rent bungalows, has facilities where we can wash clothes that undoubtedly is already badly in need of cleaning.

We ignore the guide that indicates that the day goes from Estella to Torres del Rio because it is 29 km. We preferred instead to stay in Arcos which is 21 km away, more than enough distance.

After a long walk between fields, well signposted by the landmarks, we made a stop in Villamayor de Monjardín to see its interesting church with its amiable parish priest. We have two hours of walking so we sealed the credential, had a sandwich and some water, and to continued the journey.

More fields, in the midst of which and in the shadow of the only tree in sight, we found a couple of itinerant musicians who, with accordion at the ready, start off with a typical Spanish song on the arrival of some walkers. A little later, in the middle of a field, a trailer-bar surrounded by walkers appears like a mirage. It is impossible not to stop for a drink and something to eat.

Los Arcos seemed empty when we arrived. A sign on the door of the imposing church of Santa María informs us it is closed, and will open at 5pm in the afternoon for the pilgrims' mass. Well, it's time to rest and enjoy a good meal and this seems a very appropriate place. Tomorrow will be another day.

It is common to find magical places, such as the ruins of the church of San Pedro in Viana

Stage 7. Los Arcos - Viana

Today we will complete the 9 km. that yesterday we did undertake to reach Torres del Rio, and then we will continue to Viana which is 10.5 km; a total 19.5 km, which is a perfect distance for a day. We will not get to Logroño as suggested by the guide, but the weather is rather cold, so stopping in Viana is an advantage rather than a problem.

We left Los Arcos in the early morning, with a few walkers at our side. It will be a lonely day. Flat land, straight road between cereal fields and vineyards, some small rises that we did not notice and some slight descents. Many moments to talk. No hurry, no pause. Greeting of « Buen Camino! » are offered when we near other walkers.

We found Sansol first, where we stopped for breakfast. At the exit of the town we see a running waiter who chases a couple of walkers who left without paying for their accommodation, who also warns them that in their haste they were going the wrong way. Laughter! Torres del Rio is son seen; we are in the middle of the day. The cairns, some with small stones on them, are marking the way with their yellow arrows.

Viana is on a promontory, and our accommodation surmounts just above everything, like a damn. With patience we climb the steep streets, a little sip of water, and soon arrive.

In the afternoon we visit the city, see the Plaza Mayor, stroll the narrow streets, visit the ruins of the church of San Pedro which has a good view of the valley that we will walk tomorrow.

Granite blocks make faithful guardians of the road

Stage 8. Viana - Logroño

Today our stage is only 10 km, with no large climbs and descends only one hundred meters in total.

The exit of Viana is a steep descent, ideal to start the day, which gives way to a flat and peaceful path between orchards and vineyards. With each kilometer the cereal fields are more frequent and extensive. Few forests offer occasional shade. A unique wooden overpass at mid-day on a road encourages the journey.

Being alert helps us see a pair of ducks in a ditch, but there is little else to notice. A day to walk and talk under a cloudy sky.

When we enter La Rioja we find, from time to time, large granite blocks about two meters high. The underpass under a road is followed by a long ascent ramp, which seems never to end.

Close to arrival in Logroño we find a modest bar, very informal, the first and the only one on the route so far, which is also an occasion to seal the credential. The road slopes down, which is appreciated.

The rest of the day is used for basic purchases like new socks, laces for boots, etc., a visit to the laundry, eat « tapas » and « pinchos », a visit to the Cathedral.

Finally we fell in love with the millennial places like the small and modest Parroquia de San Bartolomé. The silence of this magical place impresses, and it could well explain why so many people do the Camino without losing heart.

Navarrete marks half of the day,
and is a good place for a break

Stage 9. Logroño - Nájera

After the previous mini-day of only 10 km., today's is a long day of 30 km. by La Rioja fields. The intermediate point of Navarrete is the place chosen to pause and have breakfast calmly.

At the exit of Logroño, we cross a city park and enter a small forest where squirrels come to us without any fear; no doubt they are accustomed to the fact that the many walkers offer them food. Photos, of course. Later on, next to a fountain, the municipal notice « Prohibited to clean fish » makes a humorous note. A bar allows us to make a brief stop. Ducks and other birds meet us at the Embalse de la Grajera, a nice place to rest.

The town of Navarrete surprises us with two things. Firstly, the facade of the church reminds us of the temple of Petra that Indiana Jones made so popular. We enter, and there is an impressive altarpiece. We add the seal, and then go to breakfast at a bar on the same corner. There we find the second surprise, a ham sandwich with roasted peppers that tastes like blessed glory. This is not included in the guides.

The rest of the day is uneventful; flat, by vineyards, fields of cereal, a rest area to stop or shelter from the rain near Ventosa, a town that is far from the road and where we do not enter. Then we crossed a dry stream, on a very well prepared walkway. Without delay and without having eaten we looked for the accommodation at Nájera. We arrive when they are holding a medieval market, a pity that we cannot carry the backpack with cheese and other food.

We have left behind the Navarrese forests, the Rioja vineyards, and now under a bright sky a thousand shades of green cereal fields accompany us..

Stage 10. Nájera - Santo Domingo de la Calzada

This stage is about 20 km. in plain, and the forecast is for sun, a perfect stage. We soon depart from Nájera, almost alone. There is frost in the fields, a slope just at the beginning, a dead hare in the middle of the road, and paved road to Azofra.

A huge stone cross (a pillory according to the guide) nearly 10 meters high is on our right with banks around is the place chosen for the breakfast.

Immense cereal fields surround us, a thousand shades of green under a cold blue sky. It is easy to see the walkers who precede us and those who follow us miles away.

Moment of photographs, why not? Although there is nothing special around, with green fields, a blue sky and the silence of a light breeze - is it not wonderful?

It is almost noon, and we continue with the hats and scarves around our necks. The sun is not hot, and the gentle wind that comes from the still snow-capped mountains reminds us that we have not yet passed the winter.

Shortly before Ciriñuela, the elegant bar of a golf course allows us to sit down and take another break. We drop our backpacks with great pleasure, take a simple hot coffee with a donut, go to the toilet; in short, we recover our energy for the final stretch.

More fields, more sky, more footprints that follow us, the city, and finally our room in the Parador Nacional de Santo Domingo.

The road winds through green fields towards
the town that awaits on the horizon

Stage 11. Sto.Domingo de la Calzada - Belorado

A full day of rest in Santo Domingo, lets us visit the cathedral, churches, squares and streets. Many houses are in ruins, as under the city there is a stream that sinks the foundations of the houses and cracks the walls. The cathedral with the bell tower has separated a few meters; the two previous towers fell.

Morning dawns like many others. Despite the mists and cold, many people are assembled to start on a path to the horizon. Serene faces advance in silence, as if following a call, with little conversation.

The day advances, step by step, slowly among the eternal fields. It is not yet noon when shortly before Redecilla del Camino a large sign with a map announces that we have left La Rioja to enter Castilla. The landscape does not change, as neither the fields nor the sky, nor the road understand borders.

There are no trees, not even bushes, no birds, no ants. There are no people working the fields. We do not see anyone. We are alone, alone, alone. We take pictures of each other, why not? We are the only figures in the landscape.

At Villamayor del Río, just before Belorado, is a bar with a garden next to the road that tempts us to stop to eat. It is hot, we are tired, stopping is a wise decision. The hotel at Belorado can wait.

In the afternoon a quiet visit to Belorado, some small purchases, a light dinner at a bar in the Plaza de San Pedro and soon to the hotel to rest well.

Walking among cows or oxen is disturbing,
although they do not pay us any attention

Stage 12. Belorado - Agés

Dawn brings a cold day of close fog; after a short breakfast we start out on the road. A day of 27 km awaits us, with forests, mountains, slopes and descents, with a difference in height of 400 meters. Good mood, and a good path.

Shortly after leaving, we cross a river using a pedestrian bridge. The fog is still thick but does not prevent walking. The road is lined with yellow rapeseed fields of yellow flowers, we advance through the fog. If there is fog, we take pictures of the fog. We see the imposing profile of the church of Villambistia to the right of the road, it is closed. Later another great church at the foot of the road in the village of Villafranca Montes de Oca, also closed.

The fields are finished, we enter a dense and close forest. Traces of an animal of the family of deer, or perhaps wild boar, many beetles, green and bright frogs, trees, bushes, cows, climbs, descents, fog disappeared, it is hot, a dry heat. Gray day, we move along a path that could serve as a firebreak because it is so wide.

When we arrive at the San Juan de Ortega Sanctuary it is time to eat, we seal the credential, there is a picnic area, we buy water and we continue because we prefer to arrive at Agés rather than stopping.

We arrived at Agés, it is a bit late but we eat, we eat well, nice conversation with the owners of the accommodation and the restaurant, no more customers, drizzle, end of the day.

Slender and sober Cruz de Atapuerca,
at the end of a stony path

Amigos del
Camino de Santiago
Burgos

Stage 13. Agés - Burgos

Half an hour from Agés is Atapuerca, there is no time to stop to see the famous prehistoric human remains, besides they are not in the same town nor can they be visited without an appointment. We take note for a future visit. Some lonely? milestones reminds us that we are on the Camino. At times it seems to drizzle, but little. We decided not to put on a raincoat yet, two small oriental women who wear them put forward.

We leave the flat path between fields for an authentic small stone path that rises. At almost at the same moment we are surprised by the sign «Military zone. Do not pass» that is next to rusty barbed wire. The road passes next to the fence. Shots are heard, the warning is not in vain. Crowning the mound is the Cruz de Atapuerca, photos of course and back on the road before it really rains. A flock of sheep in an enclosure next to the road. More photos, why not?

We anticipate the sight of the oriental women, as when it starts to rain we can see their raincoats. When we don them it seems that it does not rain.

Well, now it rains, now it stops, we keep moving forward. Burgos came into sight a long time ago, but first you have to go around the airport. The day gets darker and darker. We stop to eat in Villafría, and we see how a deluge of rain falls. Could the oriental women have taken refuge? Impossible to know.

We extend the after-dinner, it does not seem that it is going to stop raining. We are already in the urban area of Burgos, so we ask for a taxi to take us to the hotel.

Hermitage, very well maintained,
closed but with a stamp for walkers

Stage 14. Burgos - Hontanas

It's still raining. We take a day off to see the town of Burgos. We visit the Cathedral, the Cartuja de Miraflores on foot, while there it starts raining, on to the Royal Monastery of Las Huelgas, closed, also on foot. There is still time in the afternoon for a brief visit to the Army Museum and the Museum of Books. The other museums will wait for another life. Guided tour of the city in which they explain their history, interesting Casa del Cordón, where the king Felipe el Hermoso died after drinking a glass of cold water.

It has rained during the night in Burgos, and continues to threaten rain, but we have to get to Hontanas where the next room is reserved. Under a leaden sky we advance along the muddy road, avoiding the puddles and with raincoats ready. There are new walkers, they are very accelerated, maybe they have started in Burgos, surely little by little they will adopt the slow pace of the march.

The first stop is in Tardajos for a mini breakfast and attend to some basic needs. To the little village of Rabé de las Calzadas, with the small hermitage of the Virgen del Monasterio next to the road.

Hornillos del Camino is the occasion for a new break, and suddenly we discover the village of Hontanas hidden under a hill when we are but a hundred meters away.

It's time to eat, shower, rest and visit the church. Luckily, the raincoats were not necessary.

Alto de Mostelares requires good mood,
calm pace and a lot of patience

Stage 15. Hontanas - Boadilla del Camino

The day dawn much covered with dark clouds, the weather forecast is scattered rains, bad news, we are sure to get wet. The guide tells us to expect flat terrain, except a climb to reach Mostelares.

We advanced under the gray sky, by narrow flooded roads because of the rain from the previous day. With care to avoid slipping we arrive at an asphalted section. Immediately we come across the ruins of the Convent of San Antón, we take a look inside but it is very squat, so we follow the path.

The ruins of the Castrojeriz castle can be seen clearly before arriving. It's also time to have breakfast, and that seems like a good place. An open church exhibits sacred art, from inside we hear thunder and it begins to rain with force. The bar is a few meters from the door of the church so we decide to have breakfast just as heavy rain starts, very happy of our good luck.

The climb to the Alto de Mostelares will be difficult to forget because a few meters from reaching the top, where there is a shelter, it starts to rain suddenly without time to put on our raincoats.

After the rain the road is even more puddled than before. Gentle descents between green fields of cereal, occasionally with raincoats.

We crossed the bridge over the Pisuerga, and entered Palencia. Near Boadilla is a tree burned by lightning, with the storm on us, we give thanks when the rainy day ends.

The morning songs of the birds on the path that
borders the Canal de Castilla accompany the walker

Stage 16. Boadilla - Carrión de los Condes

A cold day dawns, with mist but no clouds. A plain day is forecast. The sun rises behind some poplars. Photo of the sunrise. Shortly after starting, the road advances next to the wide Canal de Castilla, bordered by yellow lilies and birdsong. Several kilometers later we cross a lock, single file and holding onto the railing. It is fifty meters, looking carefully where you step, the water falls hard, place for photos. Suddenly Frómista, place of a « pincho de tortilla ».

We advance between cereal fields and stork nests, walkers in front, walkers behind, each at his own pace. Cairns and yellow arrows. Stop in the shade in a park next to the church of Revenga de Campos to regain strength. A large sign on the belfry wishes us a good path. There is not a soul. We are halfway through the day. Not a cloud, fine.

The imposing church Santa María la Blanca in Villalcazar de Sirga can be seen an hour before arriving. Standing next to it, its height impresses even more. It is closed but there is a fun pilgrim sculpture, photos and seal the pilgrim's credential. Music band and a crowd of people, they are having wedding somewhere in the town, we do not know where, but we have to continue now.

The road continues straight, flat, dry, we talk, what else can be done. Some small clouds like cottons on the sky, starts to get hot. There are not even flies. A sign announces Carrión de los Condes, the end of the day. Accommodation, shower and restaurant await us in that order. Then nap, visit the city, buy some fruit, and prepare the route of the next day.

Sky, trees, wind, sun, road, walkers

Stage 17. Carrión de los Condes - Terradillos

A new day, we crossed the bridge over the Carrión river, we passed next to the San Zoilo Monastery that the previous day we did not have time to visit, and it is written down for another occasion. We lined up with a group of walkers, we all left at the same time, the day appears flat and sunny.

We are leave behind, one after the other, the poplars to our left that are marking the way. Soon the group of walkers has completely disintegrated, each one advances at their own pace. It is said that the walkers who overcome the Palencia desert complete the Camino. The road is very straight here.

A confident and plump robin shares our breakfast at Fuente del Hospitalejo. Bread, ham and cheese, everything he likes. No doubt he comes every morning for breakfast.

As in the middle of an African desert, hazy at first, the low houses of Calzadilla de la Cueza appear. A place to pause, buy fresh water, eat, clean place, and put the original seal on the pilgrim's credential.

Near Ledigos the road forks, yellow arrows on the ground indicate the entrance to the town, but others indicate to go straight on. Two young walkers who precede us take to the town, we continue straight on the road. Soon, next to a farm of cows with precious newborn calves, we are close to reaching Terradillos de los Templarios, and then they will reach us very surprised: Buen Camino! Buen Camino!

Stone cross that marks our destination

Stage 18. Terradillos - El Burgo Ranero

For today we planned a stage of 30 kilometers, now it seems too much. We are tired, so we decided to shorten the day. Sahagún is 13 kilometers away, so in the morning we take a taxi in the hostel there and then we will walk the remaining 17 kilometers.

It is a hard day for boring, not because of the difficult terrain. The first section runs to Sahagun, a flat, straight road, without shadows, without anything in the middle of the fields, often the way is a few meters from a little-used road.

In Sahagun a plaque next to a convent informs us that we are now just in the center of the Camino French Way, which is good to know. The yellow arrows next to the bridge of the river Cea invite us to continue the journey without delay.

What follows are kilometers and miles of a straight, flat and wide road next to an endless row of young trees. Unfortunately the trees only give shade on the road in the afternoon, which is when almost nobody is walking, so if the day is sunny... then patience and keep going. A stone cross gives us the opportunity to drink some water and take a picture.

Anyone passing through the highway from León to Burgos can see on their right that endless row of young trees, and if it is in the morning they will undoubtedly see some hard-working walkers.

Upon arrival at Burgo Ranero a new stone cross welcomes us, photo of course, and seek our accommodation.

The stones piled up along the road indicate
to future pilgrims that it is the correct route

Albergueria del Camino
SOLEDAD GONZÁLEZ PACIOS DNI 969.0206-F
C/ CONCEPCIÓN 12 - MANSILLA DE LAS MULAS (LEÓN)

Stage 19. El Burgo - Mansilla de las Mulas

The small anecdotes are happening. For some stages our stops coincide with those of a Belgian couple, greetings at the stops along the way and mutual encouragement. In the restaurant of El Burgo Ranero, excellent food and good price, very kind, they give the customers a craft pin, a small yellow arrow, that craft pin will come to Santiago with us.

The guide indicates 37 km. from El Burgo Ranero to León, which is outrageously long. Better is to divide it into two sections, with an intermediate stop for example in Mansilla de las Mulas.

Fields and more cereal fields follow one another, a distant alley indicates where a river should pass. There is no cell phone coverage, but you do not need GPS to see the road, straight as an arrow, completely flat, and marked every so often by landmarks with the yellow arrow.

There is no place to stop until reaching Reliegos, 13 km away, neither towns nor small villages. At the entrance to Reliegos there is a bar, fresh water, exquisite « pincho de tortilla », coffee, toilet, and seal the credential. Following the yellow arrows we leave for the small village. The saying goes that «from Reliegos to Mansilla, a league well measured», that is 5 km., some hills, and we will arrive at our accommodation. The medieval wall welcomes us to Mansilla de las Mulas. Shower, eat in a very original restaurant, nap and then in the afternoon small purchases and visit the wall and the river, there is nothing else to do. We had dinner at the same restaurant where we ate, it's a fun place.

For urbanites it is a novelty to pass by some nests of storks and hear their unique calls

BAR RESTAURANTE
CASABLANCA
VILLARENTE (LEÓN)

Stage 20. Mansilla de las Mulas - León

Another flat day like the palm of the hand, except at the end there is a slope and its respective descent. The distance of 19 km. seems short at this point of the journey, so we delay departure until 8 o'clock. The day is sunny, not a cloud, nor are any expected. We started with good spirits, and in the cool of the morning crossed the bridge over the Esla.

Even the most anodyne day has continuous surprises, some storks on a power line, others in a belfry, blackbirds or jackdaws, snow-white flowers next to the road, a rumor, then a rumble that comes from the Eagle Patrol of the army, several pass over our heads, hasty photos.

Arrival in León, which will be a day of rest. From the hotel to the center of the city, through the Puerta de la Cárcel. Visit the cathedral, and in front of Casa Botines we see a sparkly Mirage plane parked just in front of the door, with information from an air show. Visit to the Roman wall, a museum, then another, then another, a parade of Roman soldiers in front of us. There is a Roman fair, and also the air show. We visited the Basilica of San Isidro, a saint brought from Seville, and the annexed museum where we went to see what is said to be the Holy Grail. Very pretty jewel. We visited the Sierra Pambley Museum next to the cathedral. All is right.

At dinner we meet two young asian girls, who tell us that the next day they want to see the Cathedral and at mid-morning start the Camino. We recommend they see the Cathedral that same night, have the tour, and at seven in the morning start walking.

Another bell tower with storks, with an original roof, this one in Valverde de la Virgen

Stage 21. León - San Martín del Camino

A day of almost 26 km. it's barbarous. A short, very early breakfast and quickly to the road. Plain, straight, good road, and with towns every few kilometers. Some places now start to indicating the distance to Santiago; in León a sign indicates that there are 340 km. to Santiago, less than half remaining.

We are sealing the credential, there are some places where the seal is offered, in others not. A post indicates that we are on the Vía de la Plata, good. In San Miguel del Camino a person attends a table next to the road, so that anyone can use water and cookies for free, we thank him and put his stamp on the credential. In the early hours of the day we are well prepared.

Along the way there are few places where you feel in danger, but the entrance of Villadangos was one of those. Maybe it was not a real danger, but what fear we had. Right at the entrance to the village there is a green grass soccer field, where there were about 100 black crows, and from a nearby forest came a loud sound of birds, some fluttered in the treetops. Alfred Hitchcock's film « The Birds » came to mind, and we accelerated our pace.

A bar offers « cuttlefish burgers », something similar to the typical « squid sandwiches » of Madrid. We arrived at the hostel, we did not like the ambience nor the room they offered. They tell us that there is no problem, so we we take the suitcases and go to another hostel that we saw at the entrance to the town, although there was no bathroom in the room.

.

Astorga offers beautiful monuments,
enjoy the typical chocolate of the city

Stage 22. San Martín del Camino - Astorga

We leave at dawn, we can still see the moon over the trees. At the exit of the town, the road is a narrow dirt path along which only one person can pass, for a while we advance by pushing aside bushes and brambles. It will be another flat, straight and sunny day according to the weather forecast.

Soon we arrive at Puente de Órbigo, where a panel explains its history, interesting and well explained. It seems that soon they will hold a medieval tournament with spears and horses, we take note for another occasion. It is still early to have breakfast, we continue, we join people who start the day at this point.

Gravel road between corn fields, we avoid stepping on a slug. We arrive at Villares de Órbigo, a cat on a roof looks at us curiously, a bar is next to the road, we have a good breakfast, water and a « pincho de tortilla », coffee and orange juice. Total luxury.

As we spot Astorga a couple of young walkers pass us at full speed, no problem, Buen camino!. The city is on a mound, it does not seem extraordinary until we start climbing the steep streets. In the middle of the climb, on a corner in the shade we find the couple of workers lying on the ground. Little angels, with the hot sun it pays to take things easy.

Happy arrival at the accommodation, lunch in the Plaza Mayor, curious bell tower in the town hall, quick visit to the city in the afternoon, there are many things to see. We forget to visit the Roman wall.

After a bend of the road appears the bell tower of Santa Catalina de Somoza

Stage 23. Astorga - Rabanal del Camino

Morning departure from Astorga, it will be the only descent of the day, cloudy weather, good mood. After a short time at an open hermitage, Valdeviejas, with a kind caretaker who explains the miracle that happened there to a child in a well, seals the credential.

Day of endless ascents, with towns every hour, perfect for go recovering energy. The road seems more crowded than other days, a walker woman speaks loudly on her cell phone while walking, the other surprised walkers look at her, out of tune, she is soon behind.

The fields have given way to the frequent forests that surround us. Threat of rain that tempts to prepare the raincoat. Some strong climbs on paved roads cracked by roots break the monotony and suggest going slowly so as not to stumble, we take breaks to take breath. A walker tells us that the first day near Zubiri he slipped and fell, he sprained his wrist, bad luck, but he still continue walking, Buen Camino!.

White and brown cows in a fenced field are lying in the sun on the grass, someone says that these are beef cows, they look at us curious but do not pay much attention to us. We are keeping to a good pace.

Entering Rabanal del Camino it begins to rain, we accelerate the pace, a last effort. It is a very small town, many hostels, only two restaurants and a store.

In the afternoon it rains hard, when the sky clears of clouds we continue walking through the surrounding fields, there is nothing more to see there.

The Cruz de Ferro is a cross that marks the highest
point of the Camino, in the Maragatería

Stage 24. Rabanal del Camino - El Acebo

A day that starts calmly with some climbs gets complicated at Foncebadón. The road passes through a meadow where there is a herd of cows with huge horns, without fencing or separation. We take pictures of the calves, with a lot of fear. We sealed the credential in a hermitage, barely stopping.

Suddenly we see the «Cruz de Ferro» (Iron Cross) on a long stake in a huge pile of stones. Tradition says that the pilgrim must take a stone from his house and throw it here. I cannot calculate how many stones there are, maybe twenty tones. From two coaches comes a crowd of kids who go like an arrow towards the cross to leave their stone. A teacher explains that every year they come from Murcia with the children to do some stages of the road. We leave before them.

Shortly after Manjarín, just at the end of a long hill, a mobile bar appears like a mirage, we buy water and bananas. It looks like a refreshment post for a cycling race. From now on, the rest of the day is downhill. A sign indicates a detour for cyclists, that warns us that the road will become very difficult for walkers.

From the top of the mountain we can see flags in the middle of the mountains that indicate where our accommodation is in El Acebo, and further still what must be Ponferrada.

Walk the 7 km. to El Acebo along a stony path, in constant, endless descent, but it has its reward: a soft bed.

How difficult it is to choose the best picture of the day, maybe this one, no, the other is better

Stage 25. El Acebo - Ponferrada

The day has two very clear parts, the first from El Acebo to Molinaseca, and the second from there to Ponferrada. Quiet day, good weather. The first section is a steep descent, and the second is flat. Shortly after leaving we are already in Riego de Ambrós, a small town of well-kept houses, flowers on the balconies, where we are tempted to make a second breakfast, but we continue.

Follow a narrow path, stony and steep, luckily the ground is dry and does not slip. The use of the cane is necessary, advancing slowly and with care as to where the feet are placed. Near Molinaseca it is better not to look down the ravine.

The still bells of the Ermita de Nuestra Senora de las Angustias welcome us to Molinaseca in silence. Ideal place to take some pictures, and then we cross the bridge. Paused for breakfast and a visit to the Church of San Nicolás. At the exit of the city, according to the guide, we have to take a detour to take a path to the right and advance along the Meruelo River in the shade of the trees. We did not find the announced detour, and therefore we continue advancing along the highway in full sun.

After a couple more kilometers we reach Ponferrada. The guide tells us to go to Campo, common sense tells us to continue straight on the road. We follow the guide, bad decision, with the midday heat each step is an eternity. On the ground there are marks every 100 meters of some competition, I calculate that to walk 800 km. one million steps must be taken. The hotel is on the other side of Ponferrada, we eat before checking in.

The rustic walls of a hermitage enclose a splendid sample of Baroque

Stage 26. Ponferrada - Villafranca del Bierzo

A day of rest in Ponferrada allows us to visit the Templar castle calmly, buy a new credential, the third. Then we go to the Basílica de Nuestra Señora de la Encina, take a taxi to the Energy Museum and another that brings us to the Train Museum. Very interesting.

The day begins on a gravel road between small plots and cherry trees. Camponayara allows us to have breakfast and take a break, then as soon as we leave, a long ramp awaits us until we cross the highway. The road winds between vineyards, a rabbit flees from our path.

At the exit of Cacabelos we crossed the Cua River, climbed a long steep slope. The path continues between more vineyards, mountains covered by vineyards. Shortly after leaving Pieros a fork in the road offers the option to continue to Valtuille de Arriba, we follow it, great mistake, terrible, as we see later the road stretches 5 km. for no reason. We will suffer for that extra hour at the end of the day. The path goes through vineyards, we discover that they are sulfating the vineyards, the misfortunes never come alone. We arrived at the worst moment, we can not go back, handkerchief to the mouth and accelerate the step.

At the entrance to Villafranca del Bierzo we are offered cherries next to the Puerta del Perdón, we arrived exhausted from having taken the detour, we need shade and water more than cherries but we are grateful. There is an octopus fair, end of the trials for the day, the accommodation has beautiful views of the river Burbia.

Highlands, mountains, forests and some old trees
form the new landscape of the road

Stage 27. Villafranca del Bierzo - Las Herrerías

There is no open bar in Villafranca when we start the day. When crossing the bridge over the Burbia we see a bar, La Guardia, that offers us sandwiches with bread from the previous day. For the hungry there is no hard bread, they say. We left the village with two huge sausage sandwiches.

The plan shows the stage is 28 km., from Villafranca to O Cebreiro, with a strong final climb. We decided to divide it in two, first to Las Herrerías, and then the infamous final climb of 8 km. Good decision.

The passage between the high mountains is so narrow that a highway, the national way and the Camino coincide, so much of the day passes under the columns of the highway.

The morning is cool and the day is not very sunny. Towns follow one another, eating cherries until Pereje, breakfast in Trabadelo, short stop in Ambasmestas, stop to eat in the bakery of Vega de Valcarce: « empanada » and beer without alcohol. We hear an oath in Galician, it sounds the same as everywhere. Many, many bars and hostels.

The Camino continues along the road. Carefully, we advance one by one watching the cars. The walkers on the left side, the cyclists on the right. Very busy. The trees next to the river do not shade the road, so we continue in full sun. We passed without stopping at Ruitelán, and soon we arrived at our lodging in Las Herrerías, our hostel is the last house, patience, a final effort. Shower and long nap, there is nothing to visit.

Walkers are shadows among the fog that covers
the mountains, land of bears and wolves

Stage 28. Las Herrerías - O Cebreiro

Although this day has only 8 km., the climb promises to be intense, so we leave as day breaks. The first kilometers are paved road, going up, then comes a narrow, steep, stony and wet road where we have to lean on our canes and move forward step by step. From time to time, a pause to take breath. This road ends when we arrive at the town of La Faba. Quiet visit to the church, open, seal the credential.

We decided to continue a little further. The path leaves the forest and advances between fields, we had breakfast in La Laguna (the lagoon) a strange name for a village on top of a mountain. Kind people, good breakfast, and then ... walkers to the road.

The path follows a moderate uphill road. We see how little by little the fog rises, and here it reaches us, at first it is a light fog, then an intense fog, and finally a very close fog, it is like advancing through a cloud.

It is full day, but it is colder than when we left Las Herrerías. We move forward without losing sight of the walker who precedes us. The road rises, calm, stop from time to time. It does not rain but the clothes and hair get wet.

We know that we have reached O Cebreiro when we see the first house a few meters away. We look for the hostel between the signs, because there are no streets. We leave the backpacks, the suitcases have arrived, it's time to eat.

The walkers, without looking back as the
Machado peota said, make the Camino

Stage 29. O Cebreiro - Triacastela

At dawn we leave O Cebreiro, the road is wide, wooded, well cared for. More than quiet it is solitary, gentle descents and climbs, and without realizing we are already in Liñares. The church is closed but cows at a barn greet us. In less than a kilometer we find the top of San Roque with a strange sculpture, photos on a foggy day. You can see mists down in the valleys, on we go. Shouts of warning to walkers who follow the road instead of the correct path that is on the right.

Hospital da Condesa appears at the perfect time for breakfast. Good breakfast next to an old loom, people, bustle. Nice church, photos.

In Padornelo we follow the cows that advance slowly in front of us that nobody dares to overtake. At the exit of the town a steep slope forces us to take several breaks. Youth is a divine treasure. We reach the top of Poio, go up, we advance to those who take a break in the bar there. The road continues on the side of the road. Suddenly, a marten runs across our path.

The road continues in the shade of the trees, towns that with only a few houses like Padornelo, Fonfría, Biduedo, Fillobal and Pasantes are left behind. On a narrow path, with walls on both sides, we find a dozen cows that advance facing us. There is no choice but to stick to the wall, put the cane in front, pray if you know how, and wait. The last three cows are very excited and there is little to be done. In the end everything is OK, just a good scare.

We arrived at Triacastela.

Imposing main façade of the Benedictine monastery
of San Julián Samos

Stage 30. Triacastela - Sarria

The day presents us with a dilemma. Take the route by San Xil, or the Monastery of Samos. The first way is shorter but more mountainous, the second is longer but flatter since it follows the Oribio River, and also passes through the Monastery of Samos. Most seem to follow the first, we choose Samos.

We start early, cool and gray day, narrow road next to the road, nobody in front, no one behind. The constant noise of the river accompanies us.

In San Cristóbal do Real, the din of the waterfall from an old mill attracts us to a place that is the very definition of beauty, at the exit of the village a cemetery invites to choose that place, dark and quiet, near the river, for our eternal rest. We continue through a leafy oak forest.

It is disappointing to take the option of Samos, arrive at the monastery at noon, only to find a sign that says that the visits begin at 5 o'clock in the afternoon.

In the village of Perros, following the yellow arrows, we passed through muddy and smelly alleys, only to discover that the best option was not to leave the asphalt road. The hermitage is closed. It seems clear that the people of the villages, the towns, and cities do not care about the movement of people who walk the Camino, they do not understand it. For their part, some of the walkers are interested in landscapes and architecture, and others for masses; but none are interested in the people who live in these places and their customs. At the moment this is so.

Some walkers explain to others the
traditional utility of a hórreo

Stage 31. Sarria - Portomarín

Sarria is the starting point of the Camino for many people. Most arrive by train, so the route to Santiago is more crowded than the previous ones. No problem, there is room for everyone. The exit of the city begins at the Iglesia del Salvador, which is right at the top of the city, painful effort in the early morning, resignation.

The day passes between paths and asphalted sections, forest areas and steps between fields, ups and downs. There are rest areas, bars and small villages every kilometer. The sandwiches or « pincho de tortilla » give rise to the local «empanadas» (similar to a pizza).

At this point of the road one is already an expert in local granaries; some are made of wood, others are made of stone, covered with tiles or slate, and used to store corn or sausages.

Between the villages of A Brea and Morgade is the milestone that indicates that 100 km remain to get to Santiago. This milestone is famous because it is the minimum distance to obtain the Compostela. To some it will seem a long distance, to those who have walked 700 km it seems a stones throw.

Approaching Portomarín there is a section marked as dangerous, they are high steps down between two walls, you need the cane to avoid slipping. After crossing the bridge through which Potomarín is reached, the walker takes 50 steps that look like the rise of a pyramid. Weighed down by backbacks and tired, the walkers overcome that last barrier to reach their lodging, at the top of the mound.

Stylized stone cross that time
adorned with a thousand gray tones

SAN JUAN
PORTOMARI·

a paso de formiga
Portos (Palas de Rei)

Stage 32. Portomarín - Palas de Rei

In the darkness of the early morning it is surprising to see, from the window of the room, small white lights that advance along the road. They are the lanterns of the first walkers who have already left. They must be walkers who already have the plane ticket back, and if they are delayed they must recover the lost time to arrive on the scheduled date.

When the less early risers leave we find a dense fog, and so we move along a wide path on a slight slope, between a leafy forest, a scene made for photos. You can sense some granaries in the fog. Stop at a bar in Gonzar, a crowd competes for some food and a free toilet. Fast service, good food and friendly staff.

Two stone crosses within walking distance, one shortly before Ligonde in a rest area, and another next to the cemetery of Lestedo. We continue.

In Portos, an hour from Palas de Rei, a brief stop at a bar with huge iron ants, we make the midday meal, « empanada » and drinks. Seal the credential and rest.

Soon we see pilgrims on horseback, surely they will arrive in Santiago in two days. They go without luggage, so they have a support car. Buen Camino!

The last stretch to Palas de Rei is a pleasant, flat, wide walk, in the shade of the trees, and we are already well fed.

Guardia Civil (Police) on horseback in Furelos,
a novelty for walkers

PARROQUIA
STA. MARIA DO LEBOREIRO
MELIDE

Stage 33. Palas de Rei - A Fraga Alta

The dinner in Palas de Rei yesterday gave us an unpleasant surprise, a Galician soup watery, in poor condition. Complaints to the waiter, apologies, but they still serve it to other clients. Very unfortunate.

The day begins, a cool day, an urban stretch and then the road advances through forests, photos, morning mists, more photos. There are no steep slopes or high climbs. According to the guide the day ends in Arzúa, after 29 km., but we decide to stop after 23 km. and stay in the village of A Fraga Alta.

Church of San Julián del Camino, closed, cemetery with niches to the outside. Interesting. Ponte Campaña, place of a huge scallop, exaggerated, tacky, we have a coffee, toilet only for clients. Unpleasant. We continue our way, it looks like the enchanted forest, wonderful scenery. After Casanova some cows graze quietly. The path follows the shade of pines and eucalyptus, an unmistakable scent.

Church of Santa María de Leboreiro, open, pointed arch, romanesque altar, early gothic portal, small, cozy, short stop, photos, photos.

Breakfast at Furelos is fine. We soon entered Melide, the main city of the day, which is very famous for octopus, but at mid morning, and with more than 10 km. ahead, is not time to put on the table. We continue, good way through fields and mountains. Helpful milestone, 50 km remaining. It is already a half day, after Boente there is a steep slope, arrival at the accommodation of A Fraga Alta. Leave the backpacks in the room; Galician steak with potatoes, unsurpassed.

With umbrella and cane, house robe and hat,
a woman goes to her chores

Stage 34. A Fraga Alta - O Pedrouzo

The walkers sense the end of the trip. More sadness than joy. It is almost a routine to get up before dawn, get dressed and prepare the backpack, leave the suitcase-trolley at reception, have a little breakfast, say goodbye, and start the day when the day is already clear.

The sky dawns clear, go ahead to look for the road, then a hill asks for some effort, the road advances between huge eucalyptus that hide the scarce sun of dawn.

An hour later we have breakfast in Arzúa, fried eggs with coffee, for a change. The road is marked on the ground with metal scallops. We pass by the church of Santiago de Arzúa, facade of concrete blocks, open, enter and seal the credential.

The road alternates fields and forests, asphalt and earth, slight ups and downs. The conversation decays. The towns and villages follow one another, Preguntoño, Outeiro, Boavista, Salceda, Santa Irene optional, few photos.

Many cross roads, a walker rants at a car that does not stop, it is curious at this point of the Camino. Every kilometer a milestone, every half a bar. Groups of walkers, chants, a lot of noise, bustle, people advance five by five or six by six, do not let others pass and advance like a pack. Anyway.

After a terrible final slope, in full sun, we arrived at the lodging in O Pedrouzo, first a quick shower, to eat and to rest well, tomorrow will be another day, the last day, the last, day.

From O Monte do Gozo you can see the towers of the Cathedral of Santiago in the fog

Hostal La Fuente
Teléfono
947 45 11 91
RABÉ DE LAS CALZADAS (BU)

Stage 35. O Pedrouzo - Santiago de Compostela

Early in the morning we leave the solitary village of O Pedrouzo and enter a forest of damp and leafy oaks where the morning mist is still trapped. In the faces of the walkers we do not see a festive expression for the proximity of a goal, rather it seems a certain sadness at the end of the adventure.

Young and old, whether they are walkers from Roncesvalles, Sevilla, Burgos or Sarria, they advance like they do not want to go. The milestones indicate that there are less than 20 kilometers left, a sigh.

The sun rises, we take a dirt track covered with leaf litter in the shade of a dense forest of eucalyptus. When you move the leaves, a characteristic smell rises, you breathe deeply.

Soon we arrived at the slopes of the Santiago airport, there we found a bar next to the road, it is time for breakfast, good time to take a break. A walker quickly returns to pick up the cane he had forgotten, they give him a choice between several dozen forgotten canes like his that are piled up in a corner. To the side, a church to seal the credential.

A little further on we cross a stream, very famous because it is 10 kilometers from Santiago, we do not feel like stopping or even taking a picture.

We continue along paved road, we see the buildings of local television, very new cars, here there is money.

Before reaching Santiago, we will pass through Mount Do Gozo, we move slowly, silently.

Cumplió la peregrinación
Sello.

OFICINA DEL PEREGRINO · S.A.M.I. CATEDRAL · SANTIAGO

We arrived at the strange monument on Mount Do Gozo, impossible to interpret, a souvenir photo. From there we can see the towers of the Cathedral of Santiago. The chapel of San Marcos next to the monument is a good place to place another stamp on the credential. The end is near, so close.

After the climb to Mount Do Gozo comes a straight downhill, next to a shelter for thousands of people that is now deserted.

We cross over a couple of highways and we find the first streets of the city. The sun is bright so we go from shadow to shadow. Metal shells on the ground indicate that we are on the right path to the cathedral.

Streets, alleys, squares, the mobile is indicating the way to accommodation, one last drink of water. The fresh air welcome us when we arrive at the accommodation. First a good shower, clean up a little, and find a place to eat.

Rested, clean and fed, it is time for a first visit to the Plaza de la Catedral, a photo of course that another walker takes for us with pleasure, and we go to ask for the Compostela. In the Pilgrim's Office we have a long queue, patience, we take our credentials from the waterproof bag. We check the stamps and dates. They offer us two certificates, the Compostela that is written in Latin and the other that indicates how many kilometers we have traveled, all in a beautiful red roll.

Now, all done, without hurry we can go up to the cathedral to embrace the Saint, the end of our trip.

8. The Compostela

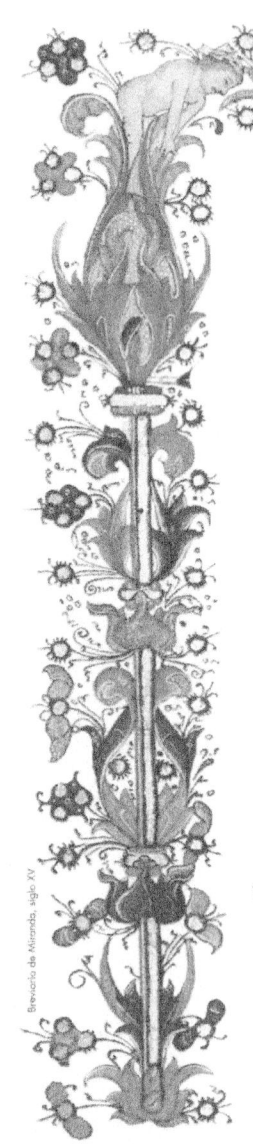

Capitulum huius Almae Apostolicae et Metropolitanae Ecclesiae Compostellanae, sigilli Altaris Beati Iacobi Apostoli custos, ut omnibus Fidelibus et Peregrinis ex toto terrarum Orbe, devotionis affectu vel voti causa, ad limina SANCTI IACOBI, Apostoli Nostri, Hispaniarum Patroni et Tutelaris convenientibus, authenticas visitationis litteras expediat, omnibus et singulis praesentes inspecturis, notum facit:

Ioannem Martín García

hoc sacratissimum templum, perfecto Itinere sive pedibus sive equitando post postrema centum milia metrorum, birota vero post ducenta, pietatis causa, devote visitasse. In quorum fidem praesentes litteras, sigillo eiusdem Sanctae Ecclesiae munitas, ei confert.

Datum Compostellae die 23 mensis Iunii anno Dni 2018

Segundo L. Pérez López
Decanus S.A.M.E. Cathedralis Compostellanae

In the Pilgrim's Office of Santiago de Compostela, based on your sealed credentials, two types of certificates are given. One is the recognition that the path has been completed, called Compostela, the second is a certificate that indicates the kilometers traveled. They also provide a cardboard cylinder to hold and protect both certificates.

During the preparation of the certificates, they ask only for basic information about the walker, such as name, nationality, motive and starting place.

In order to issue the certificates it is verified, at least in theory, that during the last hundred kilometers there are at least two stamps on the credential every day.

These certificates are the last memory of an adventure, a madness, that started a long time ago and that has filled us with positive memories.

The Camino does not perform miracles. « Quod natura non dat, Salmantica non præstat », that is: 'what nature does not give, (the university of) Salamanca does not grant', but for those who, day after day, have traveled the fields of half of Spain have the intimate pride of their prowess.

If you have done it as a penance for religious reasons, the effort you have made is obvious, if the purpose was more playful, you have shown to be in good health and have the courage of a determined mind.

9. To be continued

Millestone km. 0 in Finisterre by the ocean,
end or beginning, only the walker knows

You have reached Santiago, the end of the Camino de Santiago, congratulations. Then you visited the cathedral, the city, and you have taken many pictures. Now you have the option to continue walking to Cape Finisterre. It has come to be like a second part of the Camino, if the weather is good and you have the energy, why not? Check the guide to see the days, and if you dare ... there are four more days, ahead. You will arrive at a mythical place for millennia.

If the adventure has pleased you and you want to walk more you have three other options. One option is to return by the same path that you have come, for a pilgrim it would be the right thing, but very few people do it. The second option is to repeat the same route, surely you have found people that for whom this was not their first Camino. A third option is to start planning the Camino by another different route, there are many to choose from, long, short, you will see different landscapes, people and places.

Finally, if you want to take a long break, do so and take advantage of the fact that you are in Galicia. You can take the train and visit calmly from the beaches of the Rías Baixas to the high mountains of the Ancares, you have many options at hand. Little planning is required, either by bus, train or car, as Santiago is in the center of Galicia.

10. Acknowledgments

In memory of my faithful boots that
left their soles on the road

It is not possible to do the Camino without the help of many people. In the good times and especially in the difficult ones, it was essential for me the support of the person who dared to make the journey with me.

I also owe gratitude to the people who, along the way, treated me with care in bars, accommodations, stores, pharmacies, bakeries, churches and hermitages. His good work allowed me to enjoy the Camino.

People that I almost did not see, like the Police and the Civil Guard, but who are vigilant in the face of any difficult situation that may arise for the walker; we hope to be able to go to them in case of need. No doubt that security makes possible an adventure like this one of complete days by fields and solitary forests.

To those who write the Camino's guides. Their indications and comments have been a very useful point of reference for me first to plan the trip, and then to appreciate everything I have found in my path.

Finally I owe a special thanks to the boots that have held up stoically all the way; they have protected me from water, cold, heat and shock. Without their care it would not have been possible to complete the path.

The author

11. Basic vocabulary

The language is not a problem doing the Camino, all the staff of the accommodations and restaurants understand English, but bear in mind that only 10% of the rest of the population understands it. The street signs are only in Spanish.

During the Camino new words are learned, such as « pincho de tortilla », which is a delicious portion of potato omelette available in all the bars of the Camino.

Below is a selection of the 100 most useful words for the pilgrim.

hello, hi	buenos días
thanks	gracias
very well	muy bien
goodbye	adiós
well	bien
what's your name?	¿cómo se llama usted?
excuse me	con permiso
you're welcome	de nada
pleased to meet you	encantado
see you later	hasta luego
see you tomorrow	hasta mañana
see you soon	hasta pronto
I'm sorry	lo siento
my name is	me llamo
pleased to meet you	mucho gusto
no worries	no hay de qué
see you	nos vemos
excuse me	perdón
I'm from…	soy de…
How much does it cost?	¿Cuánto cuesta?
today	hoy
tomorrow	mañana

Monday	lunes
Tuesday	martes
Wednesday	miércoles
Thursday	jueves
Friday	viernes
Saturday	sábado
Sunday	domingo
to the right	a la derecha
to the left	a la izquierda
near	cerca
where is?	¿dónde está…?
it's clear	está despejado
it's fresh/cool	está fresco
it's raining	está lloviendo
it's cloudy	está nublado
it's nice/bad weather	hace buen/mal tiempo
it's hot	hace calor
it's cold	hace frío
it's sunny	hace sol
it's windy	hace viento
bank	banco
café	cafetería
mall, shopping center	centro comercial
historic district	centro histórico
post office	correo
embassy	embajada
train	tren
pharmacy	farmacia
church	iglesia
laundromat	lavandería
market	mercado
museum	museo
bus	autobús
taxi	taxi
restaurant	restaurante
restrooms	lavabo
supermarket	el supermercado
store, shop	la tienda
bed	cama

to cancel	cancelar
to confirm	confirmar
luggage	equipaje
single, double room	habitación individual, doble
key	llave
arrival	llegada
passport	pasaporte
reservation	reserva
departure, exit	salida
credit card	tarjeta de crédito
shop, store	tienda
water	agua
lunch	almuerzo
sugar	azúcar
drink	bebida
food, meal	comida
breakfast	desayuno
salad	ensalada
fruits	frutas
egg	huevo
juice	jugo
milk	leche
I would like	me gustaría
menu	menú
orange	naranja
bread	pan
french fries	patatas fritas
(white/red) wine	vino (blanco/tinto)
0	cero
1	uno
2	dos
3	tres
4	cuatro
5	cinco
6	seis
7	siete
8	ocho
9	nueve
10	diez

1 mile = 1.6 km.
1 USD = 0.90 euro (changes daily)

.. and remember that the greeting with other pilgrims is always: Buen Camino!

12. My own notes

Printed in Great Britain
by Amazon